This book belongs to:

____

24 23 22 21 1 2 3 4

Published by Tughra Books
335 Clifton Ave.
Clifton, NJ, 07011, USA
www.tughrabooks.com

ISBN: 979-8-89729-501-2

Mini Muslims Series ISBN 9781597849692

WHO IS Allah?

Allah is the One True God.

He is the Creator, the Most Powerful,

and the Most Kind.

He loves you more than anyone!

Allah made everything.

He made the sun. The stars. The moon.

He made the ocean. The mountains. The trees.

He made the animals. The humans.

The entire world.

He even made you!

Everything Allah made is a sign of Him.

Allah sees and hears everything.

Allah knows what's in your heart and mind.

He is always here to help you.

Allah is not like us.

He does not have partners.

We can not see or hear him.

But He is always taking care of us.

Allah loves us

And we love Him!

I ♥
ALLAH